MW00910068

Friends on my Street
A Celebration of Diversity

Erika Bracken Probst

Illustrated by Sarah Rikaz

Kennedy,
May you always
celebrate the diverse
world around you!

gatekeeper press

Columbus, Ohio

Friends on my Street: A Celebration of Diversity

Published by Gatekeeper Press
3971 Hoover Rd. Suite 77
Columbus, OH 43123-2839

www.GatekeeperPress.com

Copyright © 2017 by Erika Bracken Probst

All rights reserved. Neither this book, nor any parts within it may be sold or reproduced in any form or by any electronic or mechanical means, including information storage and retrieval systems without permission in writing from the author. The only exception is by a reviewer, who may quote short excerpts in a review.

ISBN: 9781619847972
ISBN: 9781619847965

Printed in the United States of America

Dedication

To Rowan and Sawyer for teaching me to see life through the eyes of children and to celebrate life's beautiful moments

To my husband and parents for being an amazing support in all I do

To my amazing neighbors who have given me a sense of community, and who show love and acceptance to everyone

To Everyone who continues the fight for civil rights and equality

To those who celebrate the diversity that makes each of us unique and beautiful

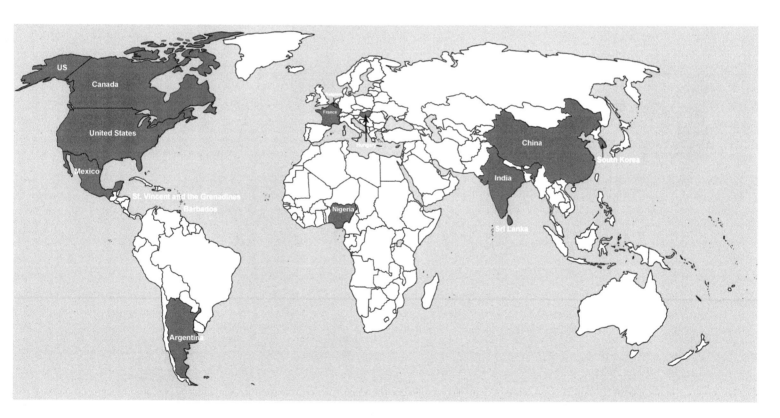

The highlighted countries are represented in this book: Argentina, Barbados, Belgium, Canada, China, France, Hungary, India, South Korea, Mexico, Nigeria, Saint Vincent and the Grenadines, Sri Lanka, and United States

Look closely to find the heart or hearts in every illustration as you read this book.

Hi! My name is Rowan. I am five years old. I live with my mom, my dad, and my brother, Sawyer. We live in Oregon, a state in the United States. The United States is in North America. My parents told me that where we live is also called the Pacific Northwest. My mom is from Alaska, and my dad grew up close to where we live.

My dad is also part of the Karuk Tribe from Northern California. My parents have promised me that they will teach my brother and me all about the Karuk Tribe as we grow up, because we are part of the Karuk Tribe, too.

One of my favorite things to do is play with friends, especially friends on my street. I would like to introduce you to some of my friends and neighbors. My parents told me the names of the countries where many of my neighbors are from. I think it is really neat that I have neighbors from so many different places around the world.

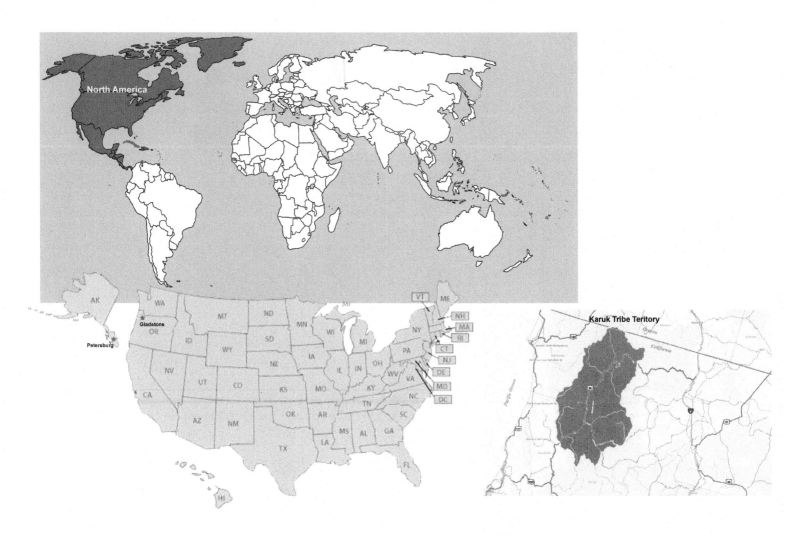

This is my brother, Sawyer. He is two. He likes to try to do everything I do. He runs a lot, and he likes to chase me. Sometimes he frustrates me, but mostly, I like him. We give each other hugs every day!

Chong lives across the street from us. She came here from South Korea. South Korea is a country in Asia, and it is far away, all the way across the ocean from where we live.

Sometimes my parents help Chong when she has questions about the English language. She likes to bring fruit to my brother and me. That always makes us happy.

Our next-door neighbor is Babu. He is from India. He told me that he grew up next to big mountains, and he had lots of mango trees! He told us we should go visit there some day, because it is very beautiful. India is also in Asia.

Babu told me he is Sikh Hindu, and he used to wear a turban on his head. He said, as a Sikh Hindu, he meditates two and a half hours every day. I had never heard the word meditate. Babu told me it is a time when he sits very quietly with his legs crisscrossed and keeps his body still.

Babu's grandson, Ashwin, lives in our neighborhood and comes over to visit a lot. He is still little, but when he gets older, I will be able to play ball with him. Ashwin's parents are friends with my parents. His mom was born in Canada, a country next to the United States, and also in North America. His dad is from Georgia, a state in the United States. My parents told me Georgia is in "The South." Ashwin speaks English and Punjabi. Punjabi is the language spoken in the part of India where Babu lived.

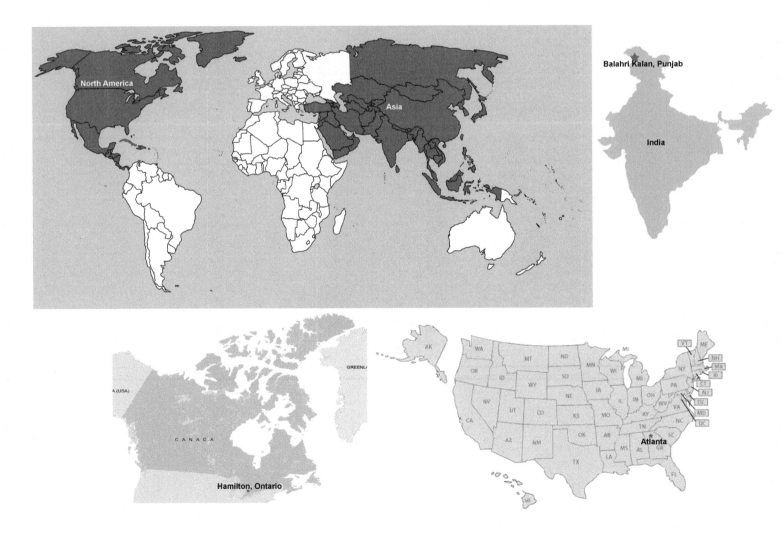

My best friend, Deon, lives on the other side of Babu's house. Deon moved here from California when he was two. California is a state in the United States, next to Oregon. We have been best friends ever since he moved here! We even learned how to ride two-wheel bikes on the same day. He lost his first tooth before me, though.

Deon has a little sister, Maya. She is only one, but she likes to play with us. Maya and my brother have fun playing together.

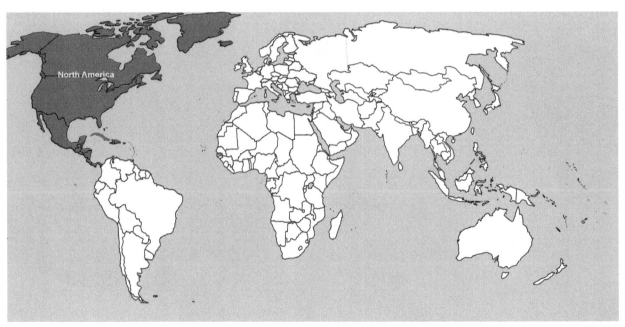

Reymone lives across the street from us, next to Chong. He makes yummy BBQ and always shares with us! Reymone came to Oregon from Missouri, a state in the "Midwest" part of the United States. Reymone told me Missouri is "Midwest with a Southern flare." I do not really know what that means, but he laughed when he told me that.

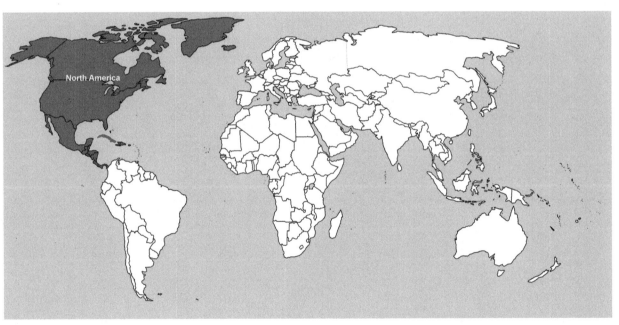

My "Auntie" Lorrie lives across the street from Deon. She was born in California, but she has lived close to here most of her life. She bakes us cookies and cupcakes all the time! She is one of my mom's best friends. They are both nurses and worked together in a hospital for many years.

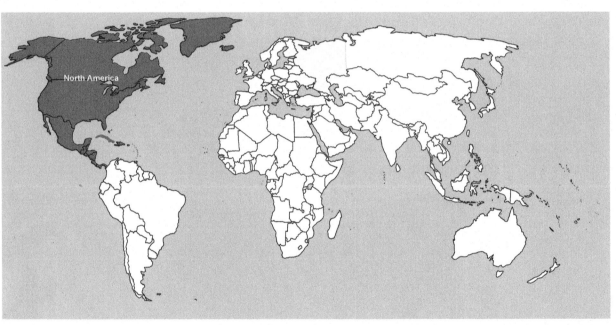

Janaya and Brenton live next to "Auntie" Lorrie. Their dad was born in St. Vincent and the Grenadines, and moved to Barbados when he was a little boy. Those countries are islands in the Caribbean Sea, and are in North America. Brenton and Janaya told me the ocean is warm there. Their mom grew up close to where we live.

Brenton is the oldest kid on our street. He is 14, so practically a grown-up. I love to watch him on his skateboard. Maybe someday I will be as tall as he is, and I will be able to do all the tricks he does!

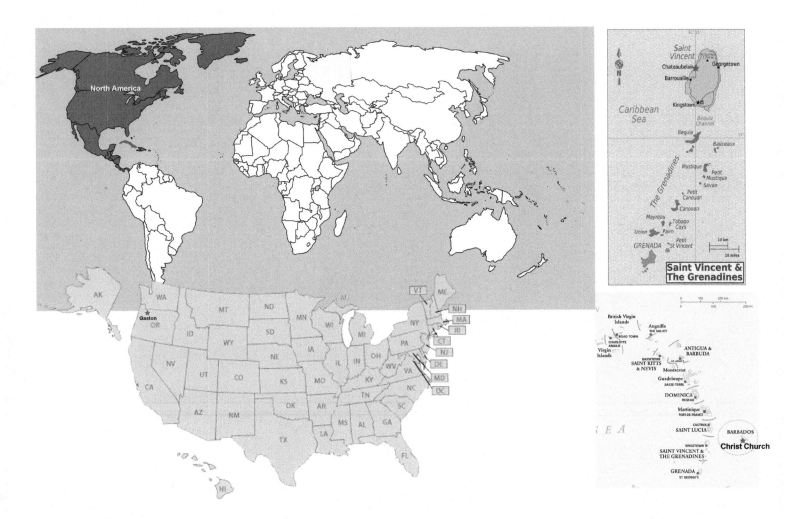

Olivia lives next to Brenton and Janaya. She is still a baby. I remember when she was growing in her mom's tummy last summer. Her mom and dad moved here from Nigeria, a country in Africa. They are part of the Igbo Tribe of Nigeria, and Olivia is learning to speak Igbo and English.

My family went to a big party to celebrate Olivia's birth. There was a lot of music, dancing, and people from Nigeria wearing clothes with lots of bright and beautiful colors. I loved all the bright colors, and I loved dancing, too.

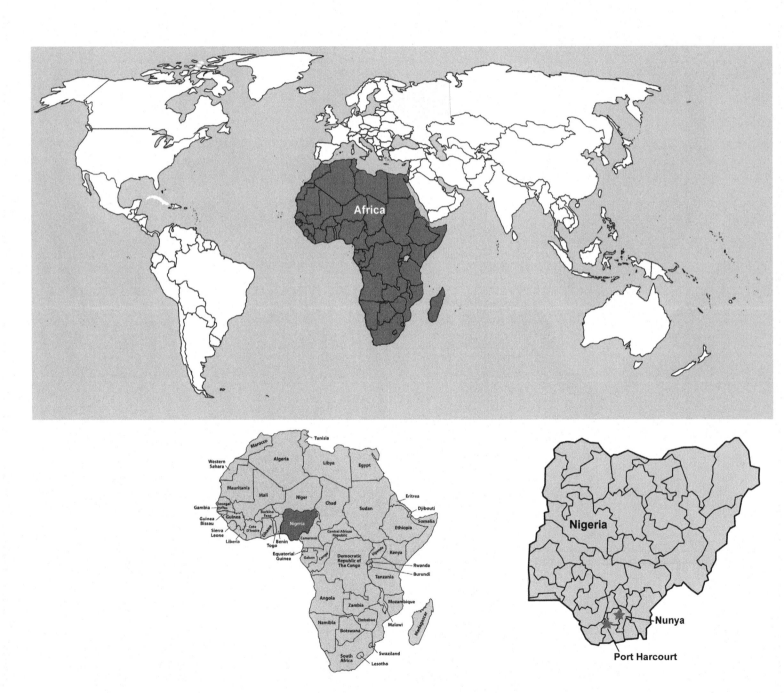

Our neighbors Chengui and Xiaolin are from China. They live next door to Olivia. China is a country in Asia. Chengui and Xiaolin take care of their grandson, Mio, and granddaughter, Jade, while their parents work. Mio and I like to play together when we are outside. He can speak English and Mandarin. Mandarin is the language spoken in the part of China where his grandparents were born.

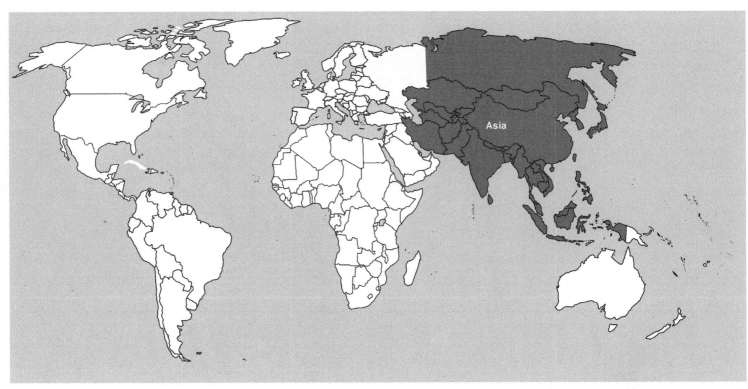

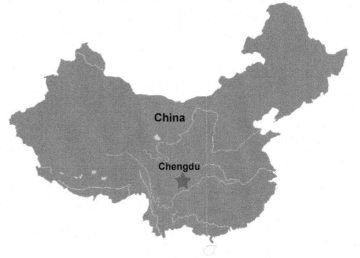

Maria and Ron live five houses down from us. Maria was born in France, but grew up in Belgium. Those are both countries in Europe. Ron is from Massachusetts, a state in the United States, but across the country from where I live.

Maria and Ron have beautiful flowers. I always like to look at their flowers because they have so many bright colors! Sometimes they give my mom their extra flower bulbs to plant in our garden so we have beautiful flowers, too.

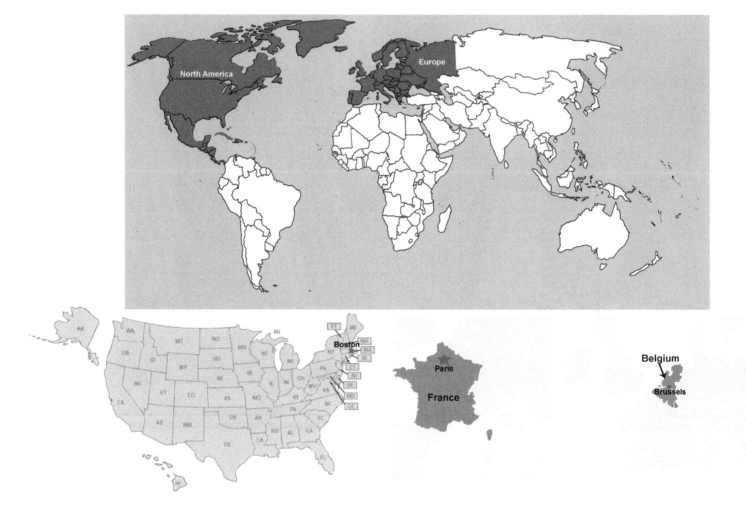

My friend, Evelyn, is three and lives next to Maria and Ron. She likes to run, draw with sidewalk chalk, and play with water and bubbles with my brother and me. Her mom is from Hungary, and her dad is from Mexico. Hungary is a country in Europe. Mexico is a country next to the United States, and is in North America. Evelyn speaks three languages: English, Hungarian, and Spanish! I think it is pretty cool that she can speak so many languages!

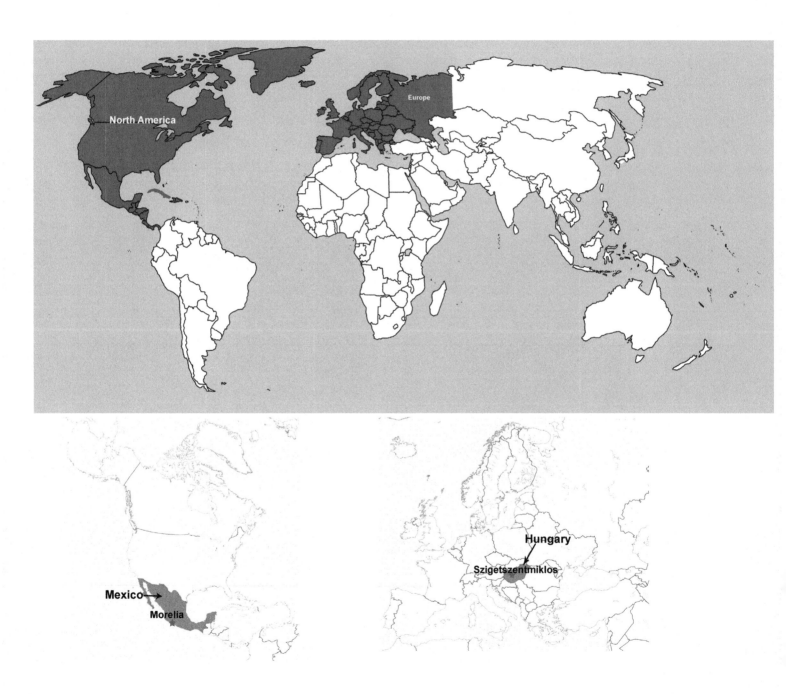

My friends Molly and Morgan live about halfway down my street. Their mom and dad both grew up in Portland, Oregon. Molly and Morgan are a little bit younger than me, but I like to play with them! Sometimes they have us over to their house for ice cream parties! I love the parties at their house because their mom always has yummy treats!

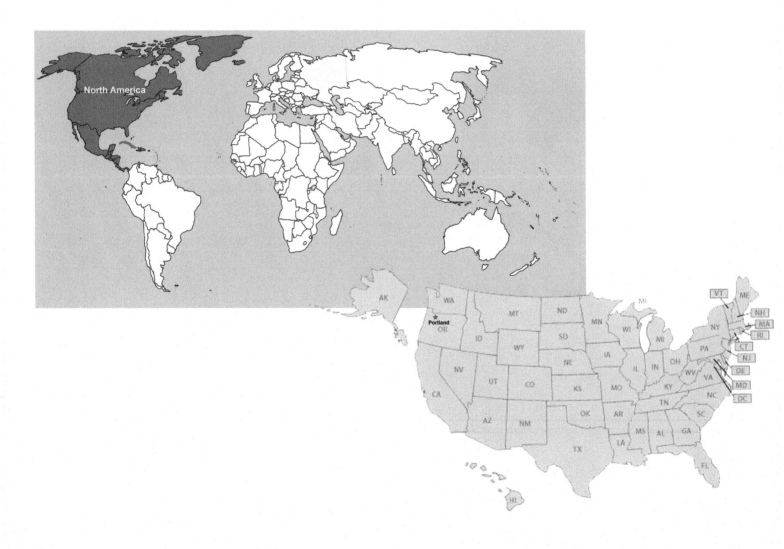

My parents' friends Diana and Elliot live next to Molly and Morgan. They moved to Oregon from New York, a state on the opposite side of the United States from where we live. They are Jewish, and they taught my mom about Kosher foods. Last year, when my dad was putting up Christmas lights, my mom asked Diana if she thought our family could put up a menorah like hers. Diana said, "Light it up!" A menorah is a special candleholder used to celebrate Hanukkah, the Jewish Festival of Lights. We put a menorah in our window to celebrate with our neighbors.

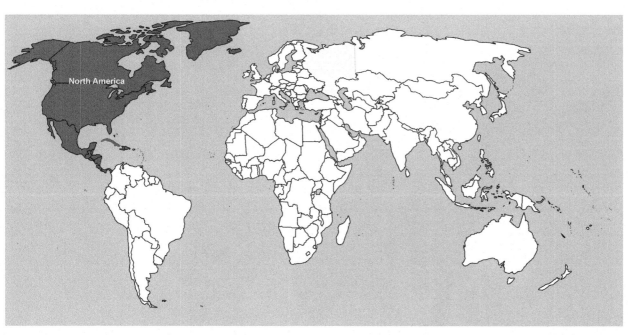

Nadiya lives a little further down my street. She turned one this winter. Her dad is from Sri Lanka and her mom is from Arizona. Sri Lanka is an island country in Asia. Arizona is a state in the United States, next to California. Nadiya is learning to speak English, Sinhala, and Tamil. Sinhala is the national language of Sri Lanka, and Tamil is the local language of her dad's family.

Nadiya's family is Muslim, and her mom wears a hijab, a scarf that covers her head and hair. My mom told me that her family celebrates Ramadan. During the month of Ramadan, they do not eat or drink anything from the time the sun comes up in the morning to the time the sun goes down at night. Nadiya will do this when she is older. My parents told me that sometimes people are mean to women who wear the hijab because they dress differently. That made me sad. I do not know why people would be mean to other people because they look or dress different.

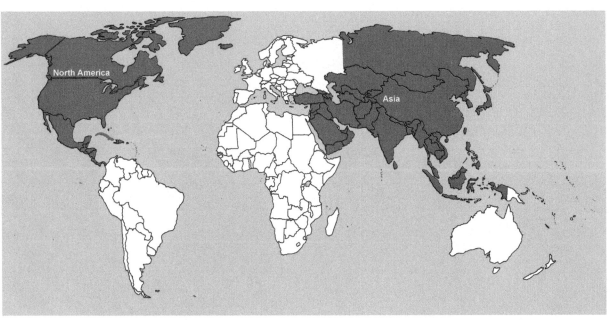

Rachel and Cole live near the end of my street. Their mom moved here from California. They are a little bit older than me. I like to watch what they do on their bikes since they can go faster than me. I try to go as fast as them! They live at their mom's house most of the time, and stay with their dad sometimes. My mom says their mom is a superhero for taking care of her children on her own.

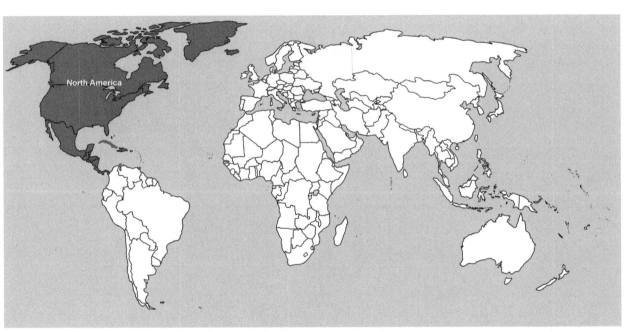

My parents' friends, Constanza and Karalyn, live one street down from me. They got married three years ago. Constanza is from Argentina, a country in South America. Karalyn is from Nevada, a state in the United States, next to California. Constanza's job is working on computers. Karalyn makes very yummy food. They are always so nice to my brother and me!

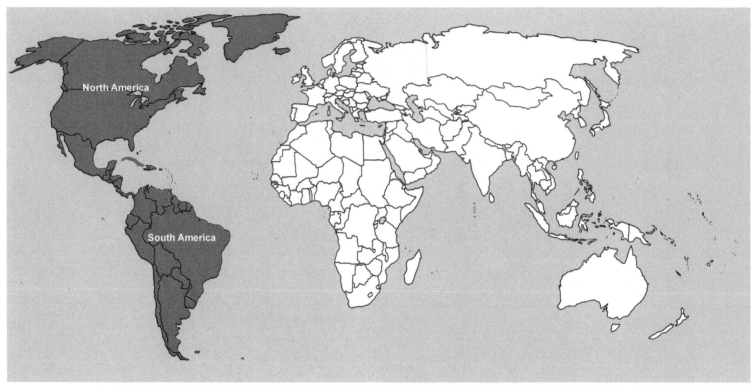

The people on my street come from many places, and we all look different from each other. We love being neighbors! We always wave and smile at each other. We also help each other out, and we even have street parties. We are all friends! I love my street!

Do people on your street come from different places, too?

Note to parents and teachers

All of the people in this story are real people, as well as their names and birth locations. We live on a short street in Hillsboro, Oregon, and we have all become very close. I hope that this book illustrates the importance of neighbors, community, and celebrating diversity. We can all learn so much from getting to know each other. We can do this by hosting get-togethers and other interactive activities like holiday parties in the winter and BBQs in the summer. The children on our street are also outside with their parents as much as possible, and we often get to know each other through our children. They are wonderful ambassadors.

As I was writing about my neighbors, I struggled with how to define each person's country or state of origin. Should I use terms describing directional locations, across oceans, etc.? Most young children are unable to grasp the concept of directions. Long distances are also hard to conceptualize. If you would like to have further discussion with your children about where our neighbors are from, I have included maps with the specific cities where the neighbors in this book were born.

According to G. Livingtson, a senior researcher with Pew Research Center, 1 in 7 children in the US today is multiracial or multiethnic. This is about three times the number of children identified as multiracial or multiethnic in 1980. It is expected that this number may actually be higher because data was based on census information from two-parent households only. To recognize and celebrate our diverse cultures and our multicultural families, friends, and neighbors is to better understand who we are as citizens of the world. (Livingston, 2017)

Reference

Livingston, G. (2017). The rise of multiracial and multiethnic babies in the U.S. Factank News in the Numbers, Pew Research Center. Retrieved from http://www.pewresearch.org/fact-tank/2017/06/06/the-rise-of-multiracial-and-multiethnic-babies-in-the-u-s/

CPSIA information can be obtained
at www.ICGtesting.com
Printed in the USA
BVOW05*0452121017
496811BV00003B/3/P